Birds
to Aircraft

Tech from Nature

By Jennifer Colby

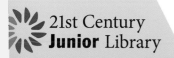

21st Century
Junior Library

Published in the United States of America by
Cherry Lake Publishing
Ann Arbor, Michigan
www.cherrylakepublishing.com

Reading Adviser: Marla Conn, MS, Ed., Literacy specialist, Read-Ability, Inc.
Content Adviser: Rachel Brown, MA, Sustainable Business

Photo Credits: © Dorian Scharp/Shutterstock.com, Cover, 1 [left]; © RamkuS/Shutterstock.com, Cover, 1 [right];
© Jakub Krechowicz/Shutterstock.com, 4; Public Domain/Wikimedia, 6; © Morphart Creation/Shutterstock.com, 8;
© Andrea Crisante/Dreamstime, 10; © Waridsara Pitakpon/Shutterstock.com, 12; © Nicky Rhodes/Shutterstock.com, 14;
© Anna Panova/Shutterstock.com, 16; © Library of Congress/Reproduction No. LC-DIG-ppprs-00626, 18; © motive56/
Shutterstock.com, 20

Library of Congress Cataloging-in-Publication Data

Names: Colby, Jennifer, 1971– author.
Title: Birds to aircraft / Jennifer Colby.
Description: Ann Arbor, MI : Cherry Lake Publishing, 2019. | Series: Tech from nature | Audience: Grade 4 to 6. |
    Includes bibliographical references and index.
Identifiers: LCCN 2018035194 | ISBN 9781534142923 (hardcover) | ISBN 9781534140684 (pdf) |
    ISBN 9781534139480 (pbk.) | ISBN 9781534141889 (hosted ebook)
Subjects: LCSH: Airplanes—History—Juvenile literature. | Birds—Flight—Juvenile literature. | Biomimicry—Juvenile literature.
Classification: LCC TL547 .C534 2019 | DDC 629.13—dc23
LC record available at https://lccn.loc.gov/2018035194

Cherry Lake Publishing would like to acknowledge the work of the Partnership for 21st Century Skills.
Please visit *www.p21.org* for more information.

Printed in the United States of America
Corporate Graphics

CONTENTS

Leonardo da Vinci designed flying machines
well before airplanes were invented.

Up in the Air

Have you ever seen a bird soaring through the air? Do you wonder what it would be like to have wings? For hundreds of years, people searched for ways to fly.

Da Vinci sketched plans for many different flying machines.

Early Flying Inventions

Leonardo da Vinci studied flight in the late 1400s and early 1500s. The Italian **inventor** watched birds closely as they flew. He built and tested many of his flying machines. But none were able to fly.

The Montgolfier brothers amazed crowds with their first balloon flights.

Joseph-Michel Montgolfier and Jacques-Etienne Montgolfier were brothers. They discovered that a bag with a heat source below it will rise. Using this discovery, they built an aircraft. They called it a hot-air balloon. This was in the 1700s in France.

Look!

What were other early flying inventions? Use the internet and your local library to research this question.

Blimps were inspired by hot air balloons.

First in Flight

On November 21, 1783, a human flew one of the brothers' creations. This was the first time a device that was not attached to the ground was flown!

Their invention led to the creation of the **blimp** and the **zeppelin**. Soon more modern aircrafts were being invented. Orville and Wilbur Wright built an airplane with an engine. Their first successful flight

Airplanes can take us anywhere.

was on December 17, 1903. Their plane flew for 12 seconds!

Today, thousands of airplanes fly every day. Airplanes carry people and goods to places all around the world. People learned how to build these incredible flying machines by studying birds.

It is impossible for people to fly by simply flapping a pair of wings, like birds. Early inventors did not realize this. Their designs failed. They did not realize how powerful birds are. Human muscles just aren't strong enough.

Birds flap their wings with strong chest muscles.

All objects in flight must deal with four different forces. They are **thrust**, **lift**, **drag**, and **gravity**. A force is a natural power that can change the speed or direction of something. Birds create thrust and lift at the same time. They do this by flapping their wings at an angle. This pushes air below and behind them.

But how does this work?

Make a Guess!

Have you ever seen a bird glide without flapping its wings? Once it has built up speed by flapping, it is able to glide. What force allows a bird to do this?

What keeps a bird in the air?

Investigating Nature

Bird wings are curved on top but flat on the bottom. Air moves more quickly over the curved tops of the wings than it does underneath. The **pressure** of the air on the wings from below is greater than the pressure pushing from above. The force of lift keeps the bird in the air.

Aircraft technology has gone through many changes.

Airplanes work in a similar way. The plane is pushed forward by **propellers** or **jet engines**. The plane gains speed until it is moving fast enough to change the pressure above and below the wings. This change in pressure lifts the plane into the air. This is how airplanes take off from long runways.

Think!

Early airplanes were made of cloth or wood. They had to be light enough to fly with a propeller engine. Today's airplanes weigh thousands of pounds! What type of engine flies something that heavy?

Jet engines allow heavy airplanes to fly greater
distances at higher speeds.

Airplanes can now fly faster and farther than any bird can. This is thanks to a few brilliant minds who looked to the skies for inspiration.

Ask Questions!

Why do you think some birds can fly and others can't? Visit the zoo. Observe the different types of birds. Take notes of their similarities and differences. Then, ask a veterinarian or zookeeper why only some birds can fly!

GLOSSARY

blimp (BLIMP) an inflated flying machine without a hard frame and shaped like a sausage

drag (DRAG) the force of air that pushes against an object as it moves forward

gravity (GRAV-ih-tee) the force pulling an object toward the earth

inventor (in-VEN-ter) someone who creates or produces something useful for the first time

jet engines (JET EN-juhnz) engines in which a very strong stream of heated air and gases shoots out from the rear and pushes the jet forward

lift (LIFT) the upward force that pushes an object from below

pressure (PRESH-er) the weight or force that is produced when something presses or pushes against something else

propellers (pruh-PEL-erz) devices with two or more blades that turn quickly and cause an aircraft to move

thrust (THRUHST) the force produced by an engine or movement that causes an object to move forward

zeppelin (ZEP-uh-lin) an inflated flying machine with a hard frame and shaped like a cigar

FIND OUT MORE

BOOKS

Fretland VanVoorst, Jenny. *Airplanes.* Minneapolis: Jump!, Inc., 2018.

Rissman, Rebecca. *The Invention of the Airplane.* North Mankato, MN: Capstone Press, 2018.

WEBSITES

National Geographic Kids—Taking Flight with the Wright Brothers
https://kids.nationalgeographic.com/explore/history/wright-brothers
Find out how these inspiring aviators took to the skies.

Smithsonian National Air and Space Museum—How Things Fly
http://howthingsfly.si.edu/activities
Learn more about the basic principles that allow aircraft and spacecraft to fly, and do some fun activities.

INDEX

ABOUT THE AUTHOR

Jennifer Colby is a school librarian in Ann Arbor, Michigan. She loves reading, traveling, and going to museums to learn about new things.